GEARED FOR GROWTH BIBLE STUDIES

TRIUMPHS OVER FAILURES

A STUDY IN JUDGES

BIBLE STUDIES TO IMPACT THE LIVES OF ORDINARY PEOPLE

Christian Focus Publications

The Word Worldwide

Written by Dorothy Russell

For details of our titles visit us on our website
www.christianfocus.com

ISBN 1-85792-888-1

Copyright © WEC International

Published in 2003 by
Christian Focus Publications, Geanies House,
Fearn, Ross-shire, IV20 ITW, Scotland
and
WEC International, Bulstrode, Oxford Road,
Gerrards Cross, Bucks, SL9 8SZ

Cover design by Alister MacInnes

Printed and bound by J W Arrowsmith, Bristol

CONTENTS

QUESTIONS AND NOTES

ANSWER GUIDE

PREFACE

GEARED FOR GROWTH

**'Where there's LIFE there's GROWTH:
Where there's GROWTH there's LIFE.'**

WHY GROW a study group?

Because as we study the Bible and share together we can

- learn to combat loneliness, depression, staleness, frustration, and other problems
- get to understand and love each other
- become responsive to the Holy Spirit's dealing and obedient to God's Word

and that's GROWTH.

How do you GROW a study group?

- Just start by asking a friend to join you and then aim at expanding your group.
- Study the set portions daily (they are brief and easy: no catches).
- Meet once a week to discuss what you find.
- Befriend others, both Christians and non Christians, and work away together

see how it GROWS!

WHEN you GROW ...

This will happen at school, at home, at work, at play, in your youth group, your student fellowship, women's meetings, mid-week meetings, churches and communities,

you'll be REACHING THROUGH TEACHING

INTRODUCTORY STUDY

LET GOD BE IN CONTROL
Do you have problems in your life which seem impossible to resolve?

Are you tempted to do things which you know are wrong and find it very hard to resist?

Do you sometimes feel a failure? Just not able to cope?

Or are you simply living the Christian life on such a low level that you no longer get excited about it?

THIS IS NOT THE WAY GOD MEANS YOU TO LIVE!
Look up Hebrews 4:9-11. The key verse is verse 10: 'for anyone who enters God's rest also rests from his own work.' What does this mean?

It means that trying to find a solution to your problems by yourself, trying desperately to resist temptation, trying to make yourself cope with life, or trying hard to be a 'good Christian' ... is NOT God's design for your life.

His plan for you is that you should have victory in every situation. But the only One who can live a victorious Christian life all the time, is the Lord Jesus. So, what we have to do is rest, stop trying in our own strength, and let God be in control. Let Him fight our battles for us.

Now read Hebrews 4:9-11 again. Does it make more sense this time?

The key thought of the book of JOSHUA is that God gave His people the land which He had promised them many years before. It was to be occupied by conquest, not in their own strength, but by faith in God.

That land was a picture of the 'life in all its fullness' that Jesus promised to all believers (John 10:10). In our lives also there are continual spiritual victories to be won and we cannot win them in our own strength. The extent to which we 'enter into God's rest' depends on how much of our lives we hand over to Jesus, so that He can rule as our King.

The book of JUDGES carries straight on from Joshua. In fact, the first few words are really the title for the whole book: 'After the death of Joshua'.

As an introduction, chapter I summarises the entry into the Promised Land during Joshua's lifetime, indicating where each tribe settled.

Now read chapter I.

The Israelites did fail to enjoy God's rest and the blessings He had promised, and failed to overcome their enemies. Only when they were really at rock bottom did they realise they were totally ineffective in their own strength, and then they cried out to the Lord. The Lord then caused them to triumph over their enemies.

The cycle of events becomes almost monotonous as we read:

3:7 The people of Israel turned away from the Lord.
The Lord let the king of Aram rule over them for eight years.
They cried out to the Lord.
The Lord raised up a deliverer, OTHNIEL.
Peace for forty years.

3:12 The people of Israel turned away from the Lord again.
The Lord let the king of Moab rule them for eighteen years.
They cried out to the Lord.
The Lord raised up a deliverer, EHUD.
Peace for eighty years.

4:1 The people of Israel turned away from the Lord again.
The Lord let the king of Canaan rule them for twenty years.
They cried out to the Lord.
The Lord raised up deliverers, DEBORAH and BARAK.
Peace for forty years.

6:1 The people of Israel turned away from the Lord again.
The Lord let the Midianites oppress them for seven years.
They cried out to the Lord.
The Lord raised up a deliverer, GIDEON.
Peace for forty years.

10:6 The people of Israel turned away from the Lord again.
The Lord let the Philistines and the Ammonites oppress them for eighteen years.
They cried out to the Lord.
The Lord raised up a deliverer, JEPHTHAH.
Peace for six years (see 12:7).

13:1 The people of Israel turned away from the Lord again.
The Lord let the Philistines rule them for forty years.
They cried out to the Lord.
The Lord raised up a deliverer, SAMSON.
He led Israel for twenty years.

In the final chapters of the book of Judges we read of some shocking incidents which were the result of the debased religious and moral standards of the times.

Judges 17:6 says: 'In those days there was no king in Israel, but every man did what was right in his own eyes.'
Judges 18:1 repeats: 'In those days there was no king in Israel.'
Judges 19 tells a terrifying story, beginning with the words: 'In those days there was no king in Israel.'
And the last verse of the book sums up the whole story: 'In those days there was no king in Israel, but every man did what was right in his own eyes.'

Consider these questions together:

1. Has our nation turned away from the Lord? What evidence do you have to support your answer? What should be the Christian's role in our society?
2. Is there 'a king' in your life? Or do you do your own thing – whatever seems right to you? (Take a few minutes with your eyes closed, and be honest with yourself about this question.)

What does it mean for Jesus to be 'king' in a person's life?

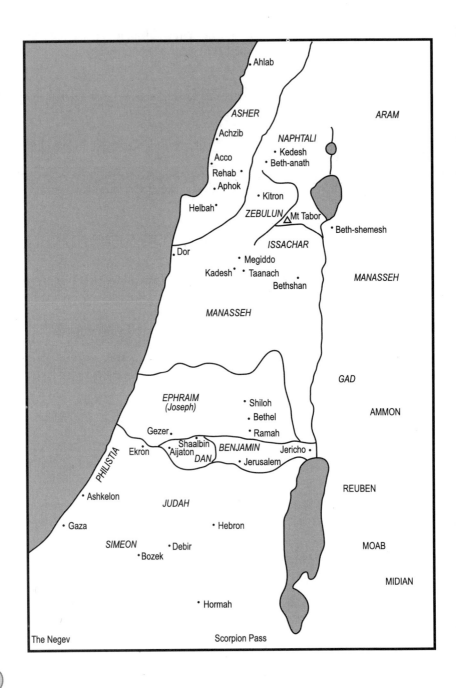

STUDY 1
THE BROKEN COVENANT

QUESTIONS

DAY 1 *Judges 2:1-5; Exodus 34:12, 13.*
a) What solemn promise had God made to His people?
b) How had the people broken the covenant? (Also Josh. 24:24)

DAY 2 *Judges 2:6-10.*
a) During what period of their history did the people truly serve the Lord?
b) Yet where did they fail with regard to their children?
c) Are you obeying the Lord's command in Deuteronomy 6:6-9?

DAY 3 *Judges 2:11-15.*
a) What was the first downward step given here?
b) What further evils followed?

DAY 4 *Judges 2:16-19.*
a) What actions did the Lord take for His people, even though they had forsaken Him? (Compare with Rom. 5:8.)
b) What does the attitude of the people show us about them?

DAY 5 *Judges 2:20-23.*
a) What two reasons are given here as to why God did not drive out the other nations in the land?
b) 'The Lord was angry.' What kind of things make Him angry today?

DAY 6 *Judges 3:1-6: Exodus 34:10, 11.*
a) Give another reason why God did not drive out the nations.
b) What blessings did the Israelites miss out on by disobeying God?

DAY 7 *Hebrews 8:8-12.*
a) What are the blessings of the New Covenant that God makes today with those who belong to Him?
b) Look up Hebrews 9:15. What is the future blessing awaiting the Christian?

'If God is a God of love, how can He send people to hell?' Perhaps the book of Judges will help us to answer that question.

Yes, God is a God of love

He is Love. We must learn all we can about the character of God, and in this week's study we see how longsuffering He is (1 John 4:8).

- He loves His people and waits patiently for them to turn to Him.
- He looks on them with compassion and pity.
- He yearns over them with infinite longing.
- He is ready to respond when they cry to Him.
- He is merciful in delivering them from their enemies.

Does He send people to hell?

No. God has never sent anyone to hell. A person chooses, of his own free will, to reject God forever. This leads to hell. When the people of Israel turned away from God and stopped worshipping Him, things went from bad to worse. They ended up oppressed by their enemies and degraded by religions which sought to appease their gods by prostitution and human sacrifices. They were living in a hell on earth. The Bible says they were in great distress.

What makes people reject God today?

They are ignorant of what He has done (v. 10).
They want to be independent of Him (v. 17b).
They are ungrateful (v. 12).
They love doing what is wrong (v. 17a).
They are stubborn (v. 19).

Human nature doesn't change much, does it? Jeremiah wrote, 'The heart is deceitful above all things and beyond cure' (Jer. 17:9).

What, then, is our only hope?

At certain periods in their history, the Israelites cried out to the Lord. As soon as they called, He was ready to answer.

It is the same today. Each person needs to acknowledge that he has been living his life independent of God, doing his own thing. The Bible calls that 'sin'. So he needs to cry out to the Lord for forgiveness.

God has made a new covenant whereby His laws can be written on our hearts. He can change us into people who love and obey Him, and who delight to do His will. Jesus called this change, being 'born again'. Forgiveness of sin and entry into the new covenant have been made possible by Jesus' atoning death on the cross, as we have seen in Hebrews 9:15. That is what He meant when He said to His disciples, 'This is my blood of the covenant, which is poured out for many' (Mark 14:24).

The book of Judges shows us the misery of people who turned away from a holy God and broke His covenant. It contrasts the sinful lives they lived with the blessings God was waiting to shower upon them. These blessings were available during their lives here on earth, yet they refused them. But anyone who rejects God in this life also misses out on an eternal inheritance, an everlasting life of joy and peace, in the presence of a loving Heavenly Father.

STUDY 2

GOD'S PROVISION FOR MAN'S NEED – A DELIVERER

QUESTIONS

OTHNIEL, from the tribe of Judah.
EHUD, from the tribe of Benjamin.

DAY 1 *Numbers 13:6, 27-30; 14:6-10, 30; Joshua 14:6-13; Judges 1:11-15.*
a) What can you discover about Caleb?
b) Who was his son-in-law?

DAY 2 *Judges 3:7-11.*
a) What did the Spirit of the Lord empower Othniel for?
b) In Acts 2:1-13 what did the Holy Spirit enable the disciples to do?

DAY 3 *Judges 3:12-14.*
a) Look up Genesis 19:36-38. How did the Moabites and Ammonites originate?
b) Who was king of Moab?
c) How long were the Israelites subject to him? (The 'City of Palms' was Jericho.)

DAY 4 *Judges 3:15-17.*
a) Look at the map on page 8 to find where Ehud's tribe lived, and shade in their territory.
b) What was unusual about Ehud?
c) How did this affect the preparations he made?

DAY 5 *Judges 3:18-26.*
a) How did Ehud arouse the king's curiosity?
b) What suggests that this is an eyewitness account of the killing?

DAY 6 *Judges 3:27-31.*
a) As Ehud rallied his men, what assurance did he give them?
b) What was the final result of Ehud's bravery?

DAY 7 a) How does Romans 6:20 parallel Judges 3:12?
b) And how does Romans 6:22 parallel Judges 3:30?

NOTES

OTHNIEL

Israel cried to the Lord and He raised up for them a deliverer. Othniel came from a godly line. He was Caleb's nephew, as well as his son-in-law.

It is interesting to read that 'the Spirit of the Lord came upon him'. In the Old Testament, the person of the Holy Spirit comes upon those whom God selects to do special tasks, and confers on them skill for their particular duty, without necessarily transforming them morally. In the New Testament, and today, the Holy Spirit comes to dwell in people, and He makes them more like Jesus.

EHUD

Israel cried to the Lord, and He gave them a deliverer. God sent a 'saviour' to save them: Ehud. He was the representative of the people, and he went straight to the cause of the trouble: the king, Eglon. It was one man facing another, and the destiny of a nation hung on the outcome.

In a similar way, later in Israel's history, the young David confronted Goliath, each of them a representative of his people. Goliath's terms were: 'If he is able to fight and kill me, we will become your subjects; but if I overcome him and kill him, you will become our subjects and serve us' (1 Sam. 17:9).

Can't you see the spiritual parallel?

For the whole of mankind God sent a deliverer, a Saviour. He was God, yet truly Man, the representative of the human race. He went straight to the cause of the trouble, into the enemy's camp, as He hung on the cross. It seemed as though Satan had won.

But as Jesus rose from the dead on Easter Day, He plunged a dagger into the enemy of souls and won the victory.

As Ehud, after his victory, blew the trumpet and called the Israelites to follow him, so the Lord Jesus calls us to follow Him, so that we can identify with the victory He has gained. In every battle we fight against temptation or our sinful nature let us remember to claim the victory that has already been won for us by our representative, the Lord Jesus Christ.

STUDY 3

THEY NEEDED A MIRACLE

QUESTIONS

DEBORAH, from the tribe of Ephraim.
BARAK, from Naphtali, with Zebulun.

DAY 1 *Judges 4:1-3; 5:6-7.*
a) Who was Jabin's commander?
b) Why was his army so powerful?
c) Discuss the condition of the Israelites at this time.

DAY 2 *Judges 4:4-7; 5:1.*
a) What can you find out about Deborah from these verses?
b) Find Ramah and Bethel (in Ephraim), and Kedesh (in Naphtali) on your map.
c) What was the message Barak received?

DAY 3 *Judges 4:6,8-11; 5:8-12.*
a) As Deborah was a prophetess (God's mouthpiece), what was Barak really saying in 4:8?
b) Describe Barak's army.
c) Where did they assemble (v. 6)?

DAY 4 *Judges 4:12-16; 5:13-18.*
a) Describe Sisera's army.
b) Where were they located? Picture the scene.
c) What is said about the Lord in this section?

DAY 5 *Judges 5:19-22.*
a) What was the miracle the Lord performed for His people?
b) Why would it have given the Israelites an advantage over Sisera's army?

DAY 6 *Judges 4:11,17-22; 5:24-30.*
a) How did Sisera unwittingly help to fulfil the Lord's prediction in 4:9?
b) Discuss Jael's action in the light of this prediction.

QUESTIONS (contd.)

DAY 7 *Judges 4:23, 24; 5:2, 3, 31.*
   a) Who won the victory over Jabin?
   b) What part did the people play?
   c) For what was Barak remembered in Hebrews 11:32-34?

THE PROBLEM

The Israelites were in a mess! They were in the Promised Land but they found themselves once more in bondage, not only to king Jabin, but also to sin. They were oppressed by a heathen people and driven back into the barren, inhospitable, mountain country. What made it worse was that they could see their enemies occupying the lush, fertile valleys below, and were powerless to do anything about it.

Do you sometimes feel powerless in your Christian life, and envy others who seem to have everything? If so, then you have a problem, too.

THE MESSAGE

I would guess that Barak was a very ordinary person (we don't hear of him again), but one who knew God as his Lord. The message he got through Deborah, however, must have shattered him. Did God really expect him to lead a suicide mission against this powerful enemy?

Sometimes, when God calls us – to take a course of action, to launch out into something new, perhaps to go to the mission field – it seems a ridiculous idea. But if we are sure of His call we can trust Him completely.

THE DECISION

Here, I think, is where Barak displays the faith that earned him a place in the 'Hall of Heroes' (Heb. 11). You might not think so when you read it first, but the courage of his decision emerges when we realise he is saying, 'I can't do this in my own strength, Lord, but I'm willing for You to use me.'

Do you ever pray a prayer like that? It's often the key which opens up a whole new way through life's difficulties.

THE MIRACLE

A number of times we read in the Bible, 'With God, all things are possible'. Do you believe this?

How crazy for that downtrodden, untrained group of Israelites, with not a weapon between them, to take on the military force of Sisera with his 900 iron chariots and myriads of troops and spear-throwing soldiers! And yet, it was God's strategy from the beginning, and He had promised they would be victorious. But how would you have felt if you had been Barak?

Then came the command, 'Arise, Barak! Today's the day!' What if he had not obeyed? If he had got cold feet? Would God have performed the miracle? I don't think so. And I believe God wants us to act on our faith, obeying His commands, even though we have no idea how things will work out.

* * *

What a thrilling story this is, the enemy routed and the land repossessed!

And Deborah? Prophetess, judge, general, singer and songwriter, she nevertheless shows true humility as she gives credit to others, and supremely to her Lord and God.

STUDY 4
FEAR VERSUS FAITH

QUESTIONS

GIDEON, from the tribe of Manasseh.

DAY 1 *Judges 6:1-10.*
   a) What caused the Israelites to be so fearful at this time?
   b) What message did God send by His prophet?

DAY 2 *Judges 6:11-24; Exodus 3:10-11; 4:13.*
   a) How do these verses bear out 1 Corinthians 1:26-29?
   b) What sign did the Lord give Gideon?
   c) What was the result?

DAY 3 *Judges 6:25-40.*
   a) How do Gideon's faith and his fear stand side by side in this story?
   b) How do you account for his courage as he assembled his army?
   c) Yet what further signs did he ask for?

DAY 4 *Judges 7:1-15.*
   a) How did Gideon show his faith in God in verses 2-7?
   b) God knew Gideon was still afraid, so how did He encourage him?

DAY 5 *Judges 7:16-25.*
   a) What strategy did God give Gideon?
   b) On what did success depend?
   c) What was the battle cry?

DAY 6 *Judges 8:1-21; Psalm 83:1-4, 9-12.*
   a) How did Gideon deal with the Ephraimites' complaint?
   b) Having captured two Midianite kings, what reason did Gideon give for killing them?

QUESTIONS (contd.)

DAY 7 *Judges 8:22-23, 34-35; Hebrews 11:32-34.*
a) Gideon's fear had become faith. How do we know this from these two readings?
b) What three things do we read about the Israelites after Gideon's death?

NOTES

Gideon is perhaps the most likeable character in the book of Judges. Many of us can identify with his reaction of fear when God called him to a specific task. His story then can help us to see how faith can overcome our fears. This is true of any situation which makes us fearful, so let's dig out the principles which we can apply to ourselves.

What caused his fears?
1. *He doubted God's word.*
   The angel's message to Gideon was: 'The Lord is with you.'
   His reply: 'I don't believe it!'

   God's message to you is: 'I will never, never leave you.'
   What is your reply?

2. *He didn't allow God's word to apply to him.*
   'Go and save Israel,' said the Lord.
   'How can I? Send someone else,' said Gideon.

   'Love your enemies,' says Jesus. 'Pray for those who ill-treat you and forgive them.'
   Do you ever reply: 'I can't do that. I can never forgive that person, much less love him (or her)'?

3. *He wanted proof that God was real.*
   Doubt – needing proof – fear: all are related.
   If you have any fears just now, check to see if you are refusing to take God at His word.

   The opposite of doubt is faith.
   The opposite of needing proof is faith.
   The opposite of fear is faith.

How did Gideon progress from fear to faith?
1. He saw God act in response to his request for a sign.
   2. He was obedient and took the first step God showed him, by tearing down Baal's altar.
   3. He saw God overrule in circumstances as his father vindicated him in front of the men of the town.

4. He was willing to take the next step and assemble an army. So the Spirit of the Lord came upon him.

5. He waited for the Lord's instructions and carried them out even though they seemed ridiculous. 22,000 men went home.

6. Again he listened to the Lord, and was willing to obey. 300 were left.

7. He received encouragement from the Lord as he overheard the dream.

8. He obeyed exactly what God told him to do, without argument.

9. He left the outcome to God. He could not have imagined what turn events would take.

10. He gave glory to God, recognising that he himself was only a weapon in the Lord's hand.

Can't you see how the Lord led him on, so that he was changed from a fearful doubting nobody, into a man whom God could use?

What about you? Check your attitudes against the ten points above. Is your faith making you a person God can use?

STUDY 5

NO-ONE MAKES A FOOL OF GOD

QUESTIONS

DAY 1 *Judges 8:29-35; 9:1-6.*
a) What steps did Abimelech take in order to become king over Shechem?
b) What was the state of the country at that time?

DAY 2 *Judges 9:7-21.*
a) What point was Jotham making by his story about the trees wanting a king?
b) What curse did Jotham place on the people because of their wickedness?

DAY 3 *Judges 9:22-29.*
a) Although the people had forgotten God, He was still there. What did He do, and why? (Gal. 6:7 is a comment on this.)
b) What was Gaal's boast?

DAY 4 *Judges 9:30-41.*
a) Who was Zebul (v. 30)?
b) Where was Abimelech living (v. 41)?
c) Describe Abimelech's tactics as he took his revenge.

DAY 5 *Judges 9:42-49.*
a) How would you describe Abimelech's actions here – reasonable? blood-thirsty? in keeping with his times? clever? those of a maniac?
b) What part of Jotham's curse in verse 20 was fulfilled literally?

DAY 6 *Judges 9:50-55: 2 Samuel 11:20, 21.*
a) What do you think was at the root of Abimelech's behaviour in this whole chapter?
b) What warning was given to soldiers in future days as a result of this incident?

DAY 7 *Judges 9:56, 57: Matthew 5:21, 22: Romans 12:17-19; Galatians 6:7.*
What lessons can you learn from these verses?

NOTES

Have you noticed that the citizens of Shechem are central in this whole ugly story?

It all began with their refusal to have the Lord God as their king, as Gideon had advised. Indeed, as soon as he was dead, they 'prostituted themselves' to idols and completely forgot God.

The next step was that they consented to have a godless man as their king, and agreed to giving money from the treasury to assist in the massacre of 69 men. Notice that God held them responsible for the slaughter, even though they didn't actually do the killing.

But – 'you can't ignore God and get away with it' as the Living Bible paraphrases Galatians 6:7.

Jotham then assumed the role of a prophet, as he challenged these citizens of Shechem with their great sin. Did he hope that some might have their consciences pricked and join him as he fled? We don't know, but none of them did.

Things apparently went well for three years and probably the citizens of Shechem thought they had been very clever. But God didn't.

So God made them hostile to Abimelech. That was all He needed to do. He knew sinful human nature would do the rest. It wasn't long before the citizens of Shechem were cursing the man who had been their hero and following a new leader.

Abimelech was quick to take his revenge and in the first combat many of the citizens of Shechem fell dead or wounded. The next day Abimelech finished them off, all except 1,000 who had taken refuge in the stronghold. But even they weren't safe from the bloodthirsty madman. They were burnt alive.

The Bible records: 'God made the citizens of Shechem pay for all their wickedness.'

What has this to say to us?

WARNING NO. 1
Remember how it all began? A refusal to let the Lord be king, and this results in someone else taking His place. This is sin.

WARNING NO. 2
God's wrath is on those who support or approve of someone doing wrong, even though they aren't doing it themselves. How do you feel about our 'permissive society'? Do you condone it?

WARNING NO. 3

God offers a change of heart at any point in time. The Bible asks, 'How shall we escape if we ignore such a great salvation?' (Heb. 2:3).

WARNING NO. 4

God's punishment for those who continue in sin is as sure as it was for the citizens of Shechem. Things may seem fine for a while, but ultimately there is eternal separation from God, with no more opportunities to repent.

* * *

Paul reminds us that we are – 'fellow-citizens with God's people and members of God's household' (Eph. 2:19).

'Our citizenship is in heaven' (Phil. 3:20).

Let us live, not like the citizens of Shechem, but in a way worthy of our calling as citizens of heaven.

STUDY 6
'I HAVE MADE A VOW TO THE LORD'

QUESTIONS

JEPHTHAH from the tribe of Manasseh (see Josh. 13: 8-11).

DAY 1 *Judges 10:1-18.*
a) Which gods did the Israelites turn to when they forsook the Lord?
b) When the people pleaded with the Lord to save them, what did they do to show their repentance?

DAY 2 *Judges 11:1-3; Hebrews 11:32-34.*
a) What effect might such a childhood have on any young man?
b) What is Jephthah remembered for in Hebrews?

DAY 3 *Judges 11:4-11.*
a) How is Jephthah's reply in verse 7 like God's reply in 10:13?
b) How did Jephthah display his faith in the Lord in these verses?
(Considering the state of the nation, Day 1, isn't this remarkable?)

DAY 4 *Judges 11:12-28.*
a) What reason did the Ammonites give for wanting to attack Israel?
b) What was Jephthah's argument in reply?

DAY 5 *Judges 11:29-33.*
What was the result of what happened in verse 29?
Read the Notes for this week's study at this point.

DAY 6 *Judges 11:34-40; Matthew 10:37.*
a) Compare these two readings and share your findings.
b) How can Jesus' words apply today in your life?
c) What can you discover about Jephthah's daughter from these verses?

QUESTIONS (contd.)

DAY 7 *Judges 12:1-7.*
     a) What complaint did the men of Ephraim make?
     b) How did Jephthah discover which of the men were really Ephraimites?

NOTES

What are we to make of Jephthah's vow? To us it seems an utterly tragic story. Why? Because we have a greater knowledge of God through His Word than Jephthah had, and we know that God did not want him to sacrifice his precious child.

But this man was acting within the limited knowledge he possessed, and so great was his loyalty to God that it overcame even his love for his daughter.

* * *

Was he rash in making such a vow?

Perhaps, but think of his circumstances. During his lifetime there had never been a God-fearing leader in his country. His own people had embraced every kind of sordid, degrading ritual connected with idol worship that it was possible to imagine. The cults from the various countries which surrounded Israel had infiltrated into his nation, bringing with them their evil practices.

Jephthah didn't even have the advantage of a secure home life when he was a boy. His father had an affair with a pagan prostitute and Jephthah was the outcome of that union. With no mother to guide his early days, and goaded by a jealous group of half-brothers who were the legitimate sons of his father, he must have had a devastating time during his formative years. Finally, he was rejected completely and sent packing. He lived by his wits as a bandit, a Robin Hood with his not-so-merry men.

Yet somewhere, in all the confusion of his early life, he learned to trust God. This in itself is quite surprising. When approached to lead his nation into battle he replied, 'Suppose we fight the Ammonites, and the Lord gives them to me ...?'

When the matter was settled, what did he do? He took the elders of Gilead to a sacred spot, and in a solemn ceremony before God, sealed the agreement. The Lord God would be his witness, his leader, his deliverer.

* * *

Why then did he make this vow which was to have such devastating consequences?

With all the enlightenment God has given us, how can we pass judgement on him? Jephthah desperately wanted to win the battle, for God's glory and for his people's good. He also wanted to show his gratitude for what God was going to do, so he promised a thank-offering in advance. That was faith. He wasn't bargaining with God, only making a solemn vow of thanksgiving even before the battle took place. How does our faith compare with that? Do we trust God that much?

And should he have carried out his vow?

There was absolutely no question in his mind about this. To break a holy vow made to God was unthinkable, even though to fulfil it would break his heart. His utter obedience to the call of God as he understood it shows that, like Abraham offering up Isaac, he trusted God implicitly. That is why his name is on the Roll of Honour of Faith in Hebrews II.

* * *

Jephthah shows us utter dedication and commitment to God no matter what the cost. God's commitment to us resulted in His sacrificing His only Son.

With your knowledge of God's Word, just think over what He requires of you, and ask yourself if you know the meaning of true commitment, not to an uninformed vow, but to the revealed will of God.

STUDY 7

QUESTIONS

SAMSON – from the tribe of Dan.

DAY 1 *Judges 13:1-5; Luke 1:5-7, 11-17.*
a) What similarities and differences can you find when you compare these two stories?
b) What was God's plan for Manoah's child?

DAY 2 *Judges 13:6-12; Numbers 6:1-6.*
a) What were the four rules a Nazarite had to observe?
b) What question did Manoah ask, which all Christian parents should ask the Lord?

DAY 3 *Judges 13:13-22; Hebrews 13:2.*
a) What lesson can we learn from Manoah's hospitality?
b) What made Manoah realise he had seen the angel of the Lord?

DAY 4 *Judges 13:23-25.*
a) From the whole of this chapter, what can you find out about Manoah's wife?
b) What advantages did Samson have as a start to his life?

DAY 5 *Judges 14:1-7; Deuteronomy 7:1-4.*
a) What did Samson's behaviour reveal about himself?
b) What was the result of the Spirit coming upon Samson here?

DAY 6 *Judges 14:8-15.*
a) Look back to Day 2. Which two Nazarite rules did Samson break here?
b) Why were the 30 companions so angry?
c) What was their threat?

DAY 7 *Judges 14:16-20; Romans 12:17-21.*
a) What characteristics of Samson stand out here?
b) How can you and I put into practice the Lord's commands in the Romans reading?

NOTES

What would you say are the most important influences on a child's life? A happy home, parents who love the Lord, a feeling of being wanted and loved? Samson had all of these advantages. Remember Jephthah in last week's study? He had none of them.

Samson also had amazing physical strength, he was mentally bright, and was blessed by the Lord from his earliest years. God had a marvellous plan for his life, to begin to deliver Israel from the Philistines, yet it seems that Samson couldn't have cared less about all that. He had no concern for his nation, his God, or even his parents – only for himself. He seems to have been utterly self-centred, lustful and greedy, and he used his 'Superman' qualities only to gratify his own desires.

Yet God had His hand on this man. This is one of the most incredible facts about this story. Consider these verses:

13:25	The Spirit of the Lord began to stir him.
14:4	This was from the Lord.
14:6	The Spirit of the Lord came upon him in power.
14:19	The Spirit of the Lord came upon him in power.

Next week we shall see more evidence of this.

* * *

The people who have everything – today

Who are they? The Apostle Paul tells us that Christians, truly born-again Christians who are 'in Christ', have the most amazing advantages. In Ephesians chapters 1 and 2, he tells us that:

God chose us in Christ before the creation of the world,
blessed us with every spiritual blessing in Christ,
loved us with a great love,
granted us forgiveness of sins through Christ's sacrifice,
made us alive with Christ,
raised us up and seated us with Him in the heavenly realms.

Whew! Did you realise all this?
God has a marvellous plan for every Christian's life. It is that we should

become holy and blameless in His sight and co-operate with Him in bringing others to know Him.

But we can be like Samson, in that we don't realise the blessings God has given us. We want freedom, we want to do things our own way, not His way. Don't you agree that this is often the case?

Yet God has His hand on you. If you have made that decision to follow the Lord Jesus, then He will never let you go. And He will work in your life until He brings you back to the point where you realise you need Him. That's what He did with Samson, as we shall see next week. Then you will begin to understand that serving Him wholeheartedly is the most perfect freedom anyone can have.

STUDY 8

THE MAN WHO FAILED MISERABLY

QUESTIONS

DAY 1 *Judges 15:1-8.*
a) What three ugly incidents motivated by revenge are recorded here?
b) Think of some occasion when you felt you had 'a right to get even with someone'. Look again at Romans 12:19.

DAY 2 *Judges 15:9-13.*
a) How many men from Judah went to find Samson? What does this tell us?
b) Why do you think Samson allowed himself to be tied up?

DAY 3 *Judges 15:14-20; John 16:8, 13; Romans 8:26.*
a) How many times have we read that the Spirit came upon Samson?
b) Did the Spirit change his character?
c) Compare this with the work of the Holy Spirit in the New Testament. What do you find?

DAY 4 *Judges 16:1-9.*
a) Look back to Study 7, Day 2. Which part of his Nazarite vow did Samson break in verse one of today's reading?
b) For how much was Delilah willing to sell Samson (Judg. 3:3 and 16:5)?

DAY 5 *Judges 16:10-16.*
a) What tactics did Delilah use to find out Samson's secret?
b) Are you ever guilty of this?
c) Why might we have expected Samson to realise what would happen?

DAY 6 *Judges 16:17-22.*
a) It wasn't actually Samson's hair that made him strong. What was it?
b) What is the significance of verse 22?
c) So the final vow was broken. What is the saddest part of verse 20?

QUESTIONS (contd.)

DAY 7 *Judges 16:23-31.*

  a) How could these verses be taken as an illustration of 2 Corinthians 12:10?

  b) What was the key to Samson's last victory?

NOTES

What sad and shocking stories we have read this week!

Samson failed to control his fierce anger, gave in to passion and lust, was self-confident and conceited, was totally taken in by the treacherous Delilah, failed to keep even the last trace of his vow, and finally, God left him.

What a warning for any of God's children who fail to let God control their lives!

In the New Testament we are shown the state of those who have left God out of their lives:

The god of this age has blinded their minds (2 Cor. 4:4).
They are without hope (Eph. 2:12).
They are in bondage because of fear of death (Heb. 2:15).
They have been sold as slaves to sin (Rom. 7:14).

How important it is for us to walk close to God and to help others to see how lost they are without Him.

* * *

Remember last week's notes? We saw that God had His hand on Samson, however unlikely that may seem. God continued to have His hand on him:

15:14   Again the Spirit of the Lord came upon him in power.
15:19   God answered his prayer (even though it was selfish).
16:17   Samson still claimed to be set apart to God!

And then ... God left him.
Why?
Had God come to the end of His patience with him? No. His mercy and love endure for ever. Samson wanted his own way. God let him have it. Like the prodigal son he had to come to an end of himself and, like the prodigal son when he turned towards his father, he found his father there, waiting to receive him.

* * *

What do you think of Samson? Are you disgusted with the way he wasted his life? Do you agree that he failed miserably to carry out the plan God had for him? What was that plan?

'To begin to deliver Israel from the Philistines.'

Look at him standing there, blind, in chains, a pathetic figure, an object of scorn. He has nothing to boast about now. Of himself he can do nothing. He has nothing, except his faith. Yes, faith, for he did not pull down the temple of Dagon in his own strength. He had to come humbly to his Creator and Lord, asking for His strength.

And God heard his prayer!

And God answered!

So Samson did 'begin to deliver Israel from the Philistines'. And God recorded his name in Hebrews chapter 11 as a man of faith along with the great saints and heroes of the Old Testament.

What a powerful story of God's amazing grace.

STUDY 9

EVERYONE DID WHAT HE THOUGHT WAS RIGHT

QUESTIONS

The migration of the tribe of Dan.

DAY 1 *Judges 17:1-6; Exodus 20:4, 23.*
a) What did Micah and his mother do, which they 'thought was right'? Discuss.
b) Where do we get our standards today, for what is right or wrong?

DAY 2 *Judges 17:7-13.*
a) In what ways was Micah 'playing at religion'? (See also 18:24).
b) How can this happen today?
c) What is wrong with Micah's confidence in verse 13?

DAY 3 *Judges 18:1-6; 1:34.*
a) Look back to 17:6. What reason is given for everyone doing what he thought was right?
b) Why were the five spies travelling through the land?

DAY 4 *Judges 18:7-13.*
a) What report did the spies bring back?
b) Who accompanied them when they set out the second time?

DAY 5 *Judges 18:14-20.*
a) What did the Danites do, which they 'thought was right'?
b) What can you find to criticise in the young Levite's actions? (Remember, he had been acting as a priest.)

DAY 6 *Judges 18:21-29.*
a) What was the significance of putting the children and livestock in front?
b) How does the whole story show the truth of Isaiah 44:9-18?

DAY 7 *Judges 18:30, 31; Joshua 18:1; 1 Samuel 1:3.*
a) Why was Shiloh an important place? Find it on your map.
b) Micah had set up for himself an alternative to God. What alternatives do people today adopt?

NOTES

Micah was a fine, successful man, a respectable citizen, wealthy, and even religious. We might say his interest lay in three things: riches, religion, respectability.

But he had no personal relationship with God.

In his beautiful home he had his own private gods in his own private church, and there, to conduct the worship, wearing the holy ephod, or priestly garment he had made, was his own son whom he himself had consecrated. And strangely enough, he convinced himself that he was worshipping Almighty God!

John Hunter, in his book *Judges and the Permissive Society* writes: 'There are many Micahs in our churches today who also play a game called "church". They may have changed the rules a little, but basically the game is the same. It is based on the same three things, riches, religion and respectability. They still build houses for their gods, sometimes very magnificent edifices. Then in this house they plan a performance. The richer they are, the better show they can put on. The better the performance, the more respectable they become. And all the time the Word of God says, "The sacrifices of God are a broken spirit; a broken and a contrite heart, O God, Thou wilt not despise."'

Is there a warning here for us?

Micah said, 'Now I know that the Lord will be good to me.'

And look what happened!

Yet the Lord actually did do what was best for him, though it wasn't Micah's idea of 'good' at all. In one day, God took away: his riches, his religion and his respectability.

He stripped Micah of all his props, of everything that came between him and his Maker, so that he had nothing of which he could boast.

What did Micah do? Did he walk over the hill to Shiloh where the altar of God was, the place where sin could be forgiven and cleansed? Did he kneel in humility before the Holy of Holies, the place God had ordained for worship and adoration?

Unfortunately, we don't know.

But we do know that if anything has come between us and God, He wants to take it away. Maybe it will hurt us terribly, as it did Micah, and we may label it 'tragedy', or 'financial ruin', but God knows best. And He will be waiting to receive us into His arms of love.

For our God is able to do even more than we could ask or imagine. Our sanctuary is set up by the Lord, not man, and our great High Priest is the Lord Jesus who Himself is the sacrifice to take away sin.

We have seen the foolishness of a man who did what he thought was right, instead of obeying God. Let's make up our minds to be people who do only what God says is right.

STUDY 10

GOD IS STILL IN CONTROL

QUESTIONS

DAY 1 *Judges 19:1-28.*
a) List the evil things in this story, which are contrary to God's will.
b) What parallels in the world today can you think of?

DAY 2 *Judges 19:29-30; 20:1-18.*
a) Look at verse 1 and verse 18 carefully. How hard did they really try to find out the Lord's will in the situation?
b) Do you think this civil war was justified?
c) What parallels are there today?

DAY 3 *Judges 20:19-28.*
a) Verses 19-23. The first day of the war. Who was victorious? Why did the Israelites weep in verse 23?
b) Verses 24-28. The second day of the war. Who was victorious? How did the Israelites show they really were in earnest this time?

DAY 4 *Judges 20:29-48.*
a) Verse 30. The third day of the war. Who was victorious? Why (v. 35)?
b) How was the victory won?

DAY 5 *Judges 21:1-12.*
a) The people had a problem. What answer would you give to the question they asked God in verse 3?
b) Did they wait for His answer?
c) How did the people rationalise the terrorism of verses 10-12?

DAY 6 *Judges 21:13-25.*
a) Historically the book of Judges flows on into 1 Samuel. Which tribe did the first king of Israel come from (1 Sam. 9:15-17)?
b) Now read 1 Samuel 12:9-15. What warning were the people given?

QUESTIONS (contd.)

DAY 7 *Nehemiah 9:24-31.*

    a) These verses sum up the history of the people of Israel in the period of the Judges. What can you find out about God from this reading?

    b) How does it affect your day-to-day life to know this about God?

NOTES

There is scarcely a glimmer of light in the chapters we have been studying this week. They show only darkness, low moral standards, debased religious concepts, and disordered social structure.

Where was God in all of this?

He was there all right, and unlikely as it seems, still in control. But His father-heart of love was breaking as He looked at all this filth and wickedness. He had created these people, given them free will, pleaded with them to love Him and they had sunk to the depths of depravity, disobeying Him and doing only what they themselves thought was right.

Did God disown them, wash His hands of them, write them off as hopeless? Did He give up on the nation whom He had promised to make a blessing to the whole world?

Listen to His words:

> 'How can I give you up, Ephraim? How can I hand you over, Israel? ... My heart is changed within me; all my compassion is aroused. ... For I am God and not man – the Holy One among you' (Hos. 11:8, 9).

People sometimes ask, 'Where is God today? Doesn't He care? With all the evil, war, terrorism and declining moral standards around us, can we believe that God is still in control of our world?'

Perhaps the study of the book of Judges with all its sordid accounts of 'man's inhumanity to man', will remind us that God does not change. He remains in control. As He kept His hand on His people in those days and accomplished His purposes, sometimes in spite of them, so today He is working out His eternal plan for the world. In the midst of greed, hatred and violence, He is calling out people who will acknowledge a king in their lives – King Jesus. People who will live no longer to please themselves, but to please Him.

Are you one of these people?

Are you standing firm for what God says is right, in a society which has rebelled against Him and gone its own way? If you have let God have full control of your life you can be sure that He is able to keep you from falling, and to present you before His glorious presence at last, without fault, and with great joy.

ANSWER GUIDE

The following pages contain an Answer Guide. It is recommended that answers to the questions be attempted before turning to this guide. It is only a guide and the answers given should not be treated as exhaustive.

GUIDE TO INTRODUCTORY STUDY

Group leaders should be very familiar with the principles put forward in the Introductory Study. Take it slowly with your group, making sure everyone absorbs each point. The whole study of Judges will hinge on this.

When you get to the bottom of page 5, 'Now read chapter I', be prepared to do the reading aloud yourself, as there are many strange names. Group members could find the places on their maps (p. 8) as you read. The main lesson to be drawn from this chapter is that the various tribes failed to drive out the people who were living in their areas.

See verses 19, 21, 27, 29, 30, 31, 33 and 34. They therefore disobeyed God. Look up Deuteronomy 7:1-6.

In considering Question I at the end, you might like to read out Romans 1:21-32, and see if our society is guilty of any of these sins.

* * *

There may be some in your group who cannot accept that God was fair in destroying the people of Canaan. This may not come up at all as you study Judges, but if it does, the following may be helpful. It is taken from John Hunter's book, *Judges and a Permissive Society,* published by Zondervan.

'Some people today are distressed at the thought of the Israelites wiping out whole tribes of men, women and children. The thing to realise is that this basically was not warfare, but spiritual surgery.

'There are times in our hospitals when one man deliberately cuts off another man's leg, thereby limiting the sufferer's entire future lifestyle. But no one objects, least of all the man who loses the leg, because this is not warfare. It is surgery. The leg to be removed is so riddled with poison and disease, that unless a drastic step is taken, the entire body will be infected and perish.

'It was this way in the tribal inheritances. The lives of the inhabitants were riddled with diseases of evil demon worship. Not only were their minds and hearts involved in sordid, lustful religious orgies, but their bodies also were infected with the foulness of venereal disease. The Lord wanted His people to be a pure people – in spirit, soul and body. There was only one way to maintain that purity, and that was to remove the possible sources of infection.'

The stories in Judges are about different tribes in Israel. As you read the subheading at the top of each page of questions, get the members of your group to shade in the relevant tribe on the map on page 8. Identify where the oppressing Canaanites lived.

GUIDE TO STUDY 1

DAY 1
a) That He would never break His covenant with His people.
b) They had disobeyed the Lord's command, had not driven out the people, and had not broken down their altars.

DAY 2
a) Throughout the lifetime of Joshua and his elders.
b) They did not teach their children to love the Lord, nor even tell them about the great things He had done.
c) Personal.

DAY 3
a) They stopped worshipping the Lord.
b) They worshipped the various gods of the people around them; raiders attacked them; their enemies overpowered them; they lost their battles; they were in great distress.

DAY 4
a) He raised up judges (leaders); saved them from their enemies; had mercy on them.
b) They had no interest in God, only in themselves. Their sensual desires got the better of them. They were stubborn and evil.

DAY 5
a) His people had broken the covenant and had to be punished. Through the temptation the other nations provided God could test His people's obedience.
b) Helpful references: John 3:36; Romans 1:18; 2:5.

DAY 6
a) To teach warfare to those who had not had previous experience.
b) They missed seeing God do mighty works among them; seeing Him driving out the nations; living in peace.

DAY 7
a) A mutual love between God and His people; personal knowledge of Him; total forgiveness of sin.
b) An eternal inheritance. (I Pet. 1:4; Col. 1:12.)

GUIDE TO STUDY 2

DAY 1   a) He was of the tribe of Judah, son of Jephunneh. He was one of the 12 spies, one of only two who believed God would help them conquer the land. He lived to enter the land. He followed the Lord wholeheartedly.
b) Othniel.

DAY 2   a) For leading (judging) Israel and winning victories.
b) Declare the wonders of God in other languages.

DAY 3   a) They were descended from Lot (Abraham's nephew), born as a result of incest by two girls raised in a corrupt, godless society.
b) Eglon.
c) 18 years.

DAY 4   a) Jericho was in the territory allotted to the tribe of Benjamin.
b) He was left-handed.
c) He strapped his dagger to his right thigh.

DAY 5   a) After delivering the tribute he turned back and told the king he had a secret message for him. (Because Ehud's right hand was free, the king did not become suspicious.)
b) The minute detail of verses 20-23. Note: only Ehud was there!

DAY 6   a) 'The Lord has given your enemy into your hands.'
b) The land had peace, and their enemies were subject to them.

DAY 7   a) Just as the Israelites had become slaves to a sinful nation so Paul points out that unbelievers are slaves to sin,
b) Just as Israel was now enjoying liberty so Christians are now free from the tyranny of sin and have become servants of God, and enjoy eternal life.

GUIDE TO STUDY 3

DAY 1 a) Sisera.
b) He had 900 iron chariots. (The Iron Age had just dawned in the Middle East and the Israelites did not use iron until later.)
c) Cruelly oppressed, danger on roads, village life non-existent.

DAY 2 a) A prophetess, married, judge, singer, songwriter.
b) As you go through this study, look up the places on a map.
c) First, to go to Ramah to see Deborah. Next, to return and gather an army to attack Sisera.

DAY 3 a) If God was in this and if He would go with him, then he would go.
b) 10,000 men from the tribes of Zebulun and Naphtali. They were untrained and had no weapons.
c) Mt. Tabor.

DAY 4 a) 900 iron chariots and all his men (see Josh. 11:1-4).
b) At the Kishon River (near Megiddo). Israelites on the crest of the hill, Canaanites in the valley.
c) He would give Sisera into Barak's hands; He had gone ahead of His people; He routed the enemy.

DAY 5 a) There was a thunderstorm and the river flooded.
b) The chariot wheels would have stuck in the mud, the horses would have been panic-stricken and the Israelites, coming down the hill on foot, would win easily.

DAY 6 a) He ran away to the tent of Heber, but did not realise that his wife sided with the Israelites.
b) Discussion – Was she right or wrong to do what she did?

DAY 7 a) God.
b) They gladly volunteered (not all – see 5:16, 17).
c) His faith.

GUIDE TO STUDY 4

DAY 1   a) The Midianites adopted a 'scorched earth' policy, invading the land in large numbers and devastating crops and livestock (v. 5 – like locusts).
b) That their present state was the result of their disobedience.

DAY 2   a) Moses and Gideon were both weak, fearful people initially, yet God chose them to lead His people to victory over strong men.
b) The meal which Gideon brought was consumed instantly by supernatural fire.
c) The result was that Gideon believed it really was the Lord.

DAY 3   a) He had faith enough to obey God without question, yet he was afraid of his family and the men of the town, so he worked by night.
b) The Spirit of the Lord came upon him.
c) He asked for the fleece to be wet then dry.

DAY 4   a) He reduced his army drastically, obeying God implicitly.
b) God arranged for Gideon to discover that the enemy was really afraid of him.

DAY 5   a) He divided the men into three companies of 100 and gave each man a jar, a torch and a trumpet. The noise of breaking jars and blowing trumpets, combined with the sudden flares of light, unnerved the enemy (and would have caused the camels to panic).
b) From the human point of view, on the 300 men having faith in Gideon and doing exactly as he told them.
c) 'A sword for the Lord and for Gideon!' (NIV)

DAY 6   a) He gave a gentle answer, thus turning away wrath. (See Prov. 15:1.)
b) Because they had, at some time previously, killed his brothers.

DAY 7   a) He refused kingship, giving glory to God; he is remembered in Hebrews as a man of faith routing foreign armies.
b) They worshipped idols; they forgot God; they failed to show gratitude to Gideon's family.

GUIDE TO STUDY 5

DAY 1 a) He went to his mother's relatives (she had been Gideon's concubine) and got their approval; he sent a message to the other citizens, who gave him money; he hired men and massacred his step-brothers.
b) A total disregard for God; Baal-worship with all its degrading practices.

DAY 2 a) That the one the people had chosen as king was as worthless as the thornbush. Also, perhaps, that people who perform useful service have more important things to do than being king.
b) Both the people and Abimelech to be consumed by fire from each other.

DAY 3 a) God made the people of Shechem and Abimelech hostile to each other as part of His plan to punish them.
b) 'If I were your leader, I'd get rid of Abimelech.'

DAY 4 a) The governor of the city of Shechem.
b) In Arumah (not Shechem).
c) He divided his men into four groups and lay in wait at night to attack Gaal. Zebul's part was to lull Gaal's suspicions, so that Abimelech had the advantage of initiative and surprise.

DAY 5 a) Probably 'bloodthirsty' and 'those of a maniac'. But discuss.
b) That fire came from Abimelech and consumed the citizens of Shechem.

DAY 6 a) Personal. (He had left God out of his life completely. Show the effect this can have on people today.)
b) Not to go too close to the city walls when they attacked.

DAY 7 God does not let evil go unpunished; He does not want us to take revenge; we are to leave the matter to Him; we should live at peace with everyone; hate and anger are equivalent to murder in His sight.

GUIDE TO STUDY 6

DAY 1   a) Baals (male idols), Ashtoreths (female idols), the gods of Aram, Sidon, Moab, Ammon and Philistia, i.e., their heathen neighbours on all sides. (Check with map on page 8.)
b) They got rid of all these foreign gods.

DAY 2   a) Low self-image, inferiority complex, bitterness, tendency to become introvert, grudge against society, etc.
b) His faith.

DAY 3   a) He, like the Lord, reminded the people that they had previously rejected him.
b) Verse 9. He knew that if victory was won, it would be God's doing. Verse 11. He called God to witness the agreement he was making.

DAY 4   a) That 300 years earlier Israel had taken over part of their country.
b) He showed how, in fact, it had belonged to the Amorites. Israel had been attacked and after they had won the battle, God had given them the land in question. He also asked why they had waited 300 years to reclaim it!

DAY 5   In verse 29 the Spirit of the Lord came upon Jephthah and he was empowered for victory.

DAY 6   a) Personal.
b) Personal (Obedience can be costly, etc. Take time on this one, leaders.)
c) She was an only child. Like her father she didn't look for a way out, but she saw her death as part of the price to be paid for the victory won. She was willing to give her life so that her father could remain true to God.
(N.B. There are no grounds for supporting the theory that Jephthah merely committed his daughter to being a virgin all her life – see v. 39.)

DAY 7   a) That they had not been called in to help in the battle.
b) If they said they were not Ephraimites, he asked them to say 'Shibboleth', a word which Ephraimites could not pronounce properly.

GUIDE TO STUDY 7

DAY 1
a) Similarities:
The wife was childless; message from angel outlined God's plan for the child; a boy promised; to be set apart for God from birth; not to drink strong drink.
Differences:
Angel appeared to wife/husband; mother told not to drink wine/no such command for Elizabeth; child's future life's work is different.
b) That he would begin to deliver Israel from the Philistines.

DAY 2
a) 1. He was to be separated (holy) to the Lord.
   2. He was to abstain from wine.
   3. He must let his hair and beard grow.
   4. He must not go near a dead body.
b) Teach us how to bring up the boy (v. 8), and what is to be the rule for the boy's life and work (v. 12)?

DAY 3
a) Don't forget to entertain strangers. (Do you?)
b) Only the actual disappearance of the angel.

DAY 4
a) She accepted unquestioningly that God had spoken to her, and believed the unlikely message; she was overawed by the visit, and guessed she had seen an angel; she immediately shared this with her husband; she had sound commonsense in her reply in verse 23.
b) Godly, loving parents; early experience of God's presence, blessing and power; chosen by God for a great work.

DAY 5
a) He was utterly selfish, with no regard for his parents or his religion.
b) The Spirit gave him supernatural strength for a particular act.

DAY 6
a) 1. Not to go near a dead body;
   2. Abstain from wine. (A Philistine seven-day wedding would have been a drinking party.)
b) They could not possibly guess the riddle, and would have to pay out.
c) We will burn you and your father's household.

DAY 7
a) Weakness under pressure, burning anger, desire for revenge, murderous fury.
b) Personal.

GUIDE TO STUDY 8

DAY 1　a) Samson burned the cornfields, etc., with the foxes; the Philistines burned his wife and her father; Samson slaughtered many Philistines.
b) Personal.

DAY 2　a) 3,000. Even his own countrymen were terrified of him.
b) Because he knew he could break free, and could use surprise tactics with the Philistines.

DAY 3　a) Four times (13:25; 14:6; 14:19; 15:14).
b) No.
c) The Holy Spirit today convicts people of sin; guides them into truth; shows Christians how to pray, intercedes for them.

DAY 4　a) Holy to the Lord.
b) 5,500 shekels of silver (v. 5).

DAY 5　a) Nagging him and prodding him day after day. She said he couldn't love her, or he would confide in her.
b) Personal.
c) Because of his previous experience (14:17), and also because of the men previously hidden in his room.

DAY 6　a) The fact that he had been consecrated a Nazarite, and God had blessed him with strength. His long hair was a symbol of this.
b) As his hair began to grow, so his strength returned.
c) He did not know that the Lord had left him.

DAY 7　a) When Samson was weak and could no longer trust in himself, he turned to the Lord and was made strong.
b) His prayer (v. 28), acknowledging God as Sovereign and pleading with Him for strength.

GUIDE TO STUDY 9

DAY 1   a) They had idols carved made of silver and they put them in a shrine. Micah installed one of his sons as priest. All this was contrary to the laws of God.
b) Christians get them from the Bible, but others from the media, peer pressure, situation ethics, etc.

DAY 2   a) He had made his own gods, installed his own priest, and set up his own sanctuary. He was living in a world of make-believe, and ignoring the Lord's will.
b) People can 'do their own thing' and form their own opinions which are contrary to the Word of God.
c) He was depending on outward ritual, not on an inward relationship with God (see 1 Sam. 15:22).

DAY 3   a) Israel had no king (i.e. to guide them in God's way).
b) To find a place where the tribe of Dan might settle, as they were cramped for space.

DAY 4   a) The land is very good, fertile and spacious; the people are unsuspecting; God has given it to us.
b) 600 armed men.

DAY 5   a) They took all Micah's idols and religious gear, and even his priest.
b) The Levite was easily swayed to do what was wrong; he was disloyal and ungrateful to his master; he was greedy and joined in the stealing of the idols.

DAY 6   a) So that, if pursued, the 600 armed men would be at the rear.
b) Micah's idols that he worshipped were powerless to help him.

DAY 7   a) The House of God (i.e. the Tabernacle) had been set up there. (Notice that it would have been quite near where Micah lived!)
b) Suggestions: sport, possessions, work, etc.

GUIDE TO STUDY 10

DAY 1 a) Unfaithfulness; lack of hospitality; lust; lack of respect for women; rape; no concern for the slave-wife.
b) Personal.

DAY 2 a) It seems they had already made up their minds as to what they would do.
b) Personal.
c) Personal.

DAY 3 a) Benjamites. Because they had been defeated.
b) Benjamites. They wept, fasted, prayed and offered sacrifices (compare the burnt offering for atonement for sin – Lev. 1:4).

DAY 4 a) Men of Israel. The Lord defeated the Benjamites.
b) The Israelites set an ambush and drew the enemy out of the city, then attacked.

DAY 5 a) Personal. Perhaps: You yourselves have killed all the men of that tribe!
b) No.
c) They agreed the best way to get wives for the remaining men of Benjamin was to kill the men of Jabesh Gilead and kidnap the girls.

DAY 6 a) The tribe of Benjamin.
b) If they did not obey the Lord after they got their king, God would punish them just as much as He did when they had no king.

DAY 7 a) God heard their cries for help, was compassionate, and rescued them from their enemies time after time. He never abandoned them, but was gracious and merciful.
b) Personal. (God does not change, so I can be sure He hears my prayers and will rescue me from the devil's attacks. He is ready to forgive, and will never leave me.)

THE WORD WORLDWIDE

We first heard of WORD WORLDWIDE over 20 years ago when Marie Dinnen, its founder, shared excitedly about the wonderful way ministry to one needy woman had exploded to touch many lives. It was great to see the Word of God being made central in the lives of thousands of men and women, then to witness the life-changing results of them applying the Word to their circumstances. Over the years the vision for WORD WORLDWIDE has not dimmed in the hearts of those who are involved in this ministry. God is still at work through His Word and in today's self-seeking society, the Word is even more relevant to those who desire true meaning and purpose in life. WORD WORLDWIDE is a ministry of WEC International, an interdenominational missionary society, whose sole purpose is to see Christ known, loved and worshipped by all, particularly those who have yet to hear of His wonderful name. This ministry is a vital part of our work and we warmly recommend the WORD WORLDWIDE 'Geared for Growth' Bible studies to you. We know that as you study His Word you will be enriched in your personal walk with Christ. It is our hope that as you are blessed through these studies, you will find opportunities to help others discover a personal relationship with Jesus. As a mission we would encourage you to work with us to make Christ known to the ends of the earth.

Stewart and Jean Moulds – British Directors, **WEC International**.

A full list of over 50 'Geared for Growth' studies can be obtained from:

ENGLAND *North East/South*: John and Ann Edwards
5 Louvaine Terrace, Hetton-le-Hole, Tyne & Wear, DH5 9PP
Tel. 0191 5262803 Email: rhysjohn.edwards@virgin.net
North West/Midlands: Anne Jenkins
2 Windermere Road, Carnforth, Lancs., LA5 9AR
Tel. 01524 734797 Email: anne@jenkins.abelgratis.com
West: Pam Riches Tel. 01594 834241

IRELAND Steffney Preston
33 Harcourts Hill, Portadown, Craigavon, N. Ireland, BT62 3RE
Tel. 028 3833 7844 Email: sa.preston@talk21.com

SCOTLAND Margaret Halliday
10 Douglas Drive, Newton Mearns, Glasgow, G77 6HR
Tel. 0141 639 8695 Email: mhalliday@onetel.net.uk

WALES William and Eirian Edwards
Penlan Uchaf, Carmarthen Road, Kidwelly, Carms., SA17 5AF
Tel. 01554 890423 Email: penlanuchaf@fwi.co.uk

UK CO-ORDINATOR
Anne Jenkins
2 Windermere Road, Carnforth, Lancs., LA5 9AR
Tel. 01524 734797 Email: anne@jenkins.abelgratis.com

UK Website: www.wordworldwide.org.uk

Christian Focus Publications

publishes books for all ages

Our mission statement –

STAYING FAITHFUL

In dependence upon God we seek to help make His infallible word, the Bible, relevant. Our aim is to ensure that the Lord Jesus Christ is presented as the only hope to obtain forgiveness of sin, live a useful life and look forward to heaven with Him.

REACHING OUT

Christ's last command requires us to reach out to our world with His gospel. We seek to help fulfill that by publishing books that point people towards Jesus and help them develop a Christ-like maturity. We aim to equip all levels of readers for life, work, ministry and mission.

Books in our adult range are published in three imprints.

Christian Focus contains popular works including biographies, commentaries, basic doctrine, and Christian living. Our children's books are also published in this imprint.

Mentor focuses on books written at a level suitable for Bible College and seminary students, pastors, and other serious readers; the imprint includes commentaries, doctrinal studies, examination of current issues, and church history.

Christian Heritage contains classic writings from the past.